INNER WEATHER

INNER WEATHER

ROBERT PHILLIPS

The Golden Quill Press
PUBLISHERS
Francestown   New Hampshire

Dedicated to Judith:

A poet's poet

ACKNOWLEDGMENTS

Some of these poems first appeared in the anthologies *American Poetry, Old and New* (1965), *Treasures of Parnassus: Best Poems of 1963*, and *National Anthology of College Poetry* (1958, 1959, 1960), and in the following periodicals: *Forum* (Ball State University), *The Carleton Miscellany, Dust, Lance, Mad River Review, New Mexico Quarterly, New York Herald Tribune, The Poet's Mission, Signal, Syracuse 10*, and *Voices*. Several appeared, in different form, in the privately printed book *8&8* (Syracuse: 1960). Thanks is due the editors for each permission to reprint, and to Harcourt, Brace & World for the lines from Virginia Woolf's *To the Lighthouse* — the epigraph.

CONTENTS

The great revelation had never come.
The great revelation perhaps never did come.
Instead there were little daily miracles, illuminations, matches struck unexpectedly in the dark . . .

VIRGINIA WOOLF,
To the Lighthouse

THE WEIRD SISTER

There was a woman with an awful eye
who brandished a witching wand
("To beat the dogs off with!" she cried),
who walked our world even in wildest weather,
nursing within her lank arm's crook
the doll she'd fashioned from rags. Its
bright button eye was affixed
upon the faded blue-denim comforter
which was our sky. The familiar doll,
the daughter, hung limp and loveless within her
   grasp.
"Fly for us, oh fly!" we jeered,
come to their unpretty pass.

Together they travelled the country's
concourse, past children who shrieked
and grabbed at tattered skirts which dragged like
   nets
("Fly, oh fly!"), past brindled cows sweetly chewing
   grass,
centipede clotheslines flapping legs in dervish
   dance.
They travelled to where our earth ends
and the sky begins, beyond the Dead End sign
over Hasting's Cliff. ("Fly, oh fly!")

Now she has flown.
No cold mud sucks at her freezing toes.
Her high, curlew cries do not thread the winds
shuttling past windows where drowsy students stare.

The doughty daughter, maimed asymmetrical,
cast aside, sees but pities not the spectacle
of that rockpile which rose up rightly
to smash a witch who could not
fly.

SUNFLOWERS

How bold, how vivid the sunburst of your bloom!
 Yellow-rayed flowers, you proclaim the summer
With more exuberance and broom stamina
 Than all croaking frog bellies of the season.
You brandish, blazen forth your feverish glow,
 Brave blond flames meet and match August, heat
  for heat.

And how brilliantly you defy dire autumn:
 Blossoms curling like smoke puffs of kindled
  bronze,
Aglow like rust-dapplings, stains of molten orange;
 You stand stalking your ground, stiffening in the
  breeze,
The phoenix of flowers, bright pillars of fire,
 Then in umber silence — you burn yourselves out.

VIEWING

They come, who have ever loved death better than
    peace,
Better than love or the incantation of laughter;
Delighting in the size of the floral display,
Remarking how natural the painted, powdered smile.

HAPPENINGS

Rounding the blank corner of my block
I stagger under sudden shock —
Red lights flash, arched hose streams,
Fire-engine throbs, siren screams —
The head knows it is my house
Long after eyes espouse
The truth. The neighbors'.
Someone else.

Disaster rarely clangs and wails
Before one's door. It comes quietly, in the mail,
In the slight sigh of brakes that fail.
Swimmers disappear silently as the sun,
The ticker's indifferent click-click stuns,
A mote captured in the X-ray beams
Malignant. The telegram's bright collage
Does not shout, it whispers
You.

THIRTY-EIGHT SUMMERS

Helen, with her sun-dead skin
Tanned umber the three months through,
Knew desire as she knew
The scorched sands of sundry beaches . . .

Even the coldness of the outdoor shower
Pelting and pricking her conscience
Could do nothing to cool those coals.
The sound of drumming water
Against the tin shower stall
Was heavy sleet against her heart's barricade.

Helen, when walking the edge of a fretting surf
Would feel the jab of love, sharp, distinct,
Like the throb of a bare foot
That has run too quickly and foolishly
Over rough and nail-studded boards.

To look at the beach was pain enough:
Couples everywhere laughing
Beneath the saffron-streaked sky.
It made her dizzy, knotted in the throat.

Helen went crabbing one afternoon.
There was no one to help her bait
Her safety pin with the dead fish head.
How she hated the dead fish head;
Its cold insolent eye razored
Through her, into her body's marrow.

She recalled dry bleached wigs of seaweed
And raw, raw ribs of whales.

She dropped the frail line
Into dark water depths below.

For thirty-eight summers she had known
The moist cool smells of wet cement;
Nail-gouged sand and grit from her scalp.
Helen knew everything but the feel and smell of
   love,
And how to bait a safety pin hook.

LECTURE

All these quick and callous to condemn,
Pointing rigid, horny fingers, *"J'accuse!"*
At mauve tea-gowned boys on a cotquean cruise,
Lesbians with bolstered shoulders, boisterous as
  men;

Let them not forget forces antipodal which pit
Gene against gene, to transmogrify us all:
Men of muscle, androgynizing in the fall
Of weights, and violets shrinking as they knit;

That chemistry which stealthily has stolen
The voice of the old man, sea-changed, Caliope
  thin;
Caused the muliebrious pink lady to take on the
  chin
Whiskers of wire, which she toughly tholes.

PICASSO'S "BOY LEADING A HORSE"

It is a naked horse and a naked boy
Who have nothing at all in their nakedness
Except loneliness shared and dim destiny.
No one knows whether the horse mourns the evening
Or if the boy's mourning somehow touches the
    horse.

When they draw near they are always withdrawn,
Always aloof from that evening to which they
    belong.
(In the grey plane that encloses them.)

If from one or the other comes suddenly
Clarion call or lamentation, we should know
It is because it is evening for both of them:

The boy's evening comes with the first shining star,
The horse's evening with the sight of hay —
Just two in time, more lonely with the dusk.

THE WINTER OF UNTIL

Shadows. Thin, blue, sharp.
Shadows cutting crust and mummy mush.
White silence lies like a sheet over the dead,
the earth a rigid cadaver on view.
That frigid sun, an antique withered fruit,
shines but does not warm the glazed land.
The hideous muteness of a universe —
a gash in the head of a drum —
mocks the music from a lone and leaden bird.
Biting cold laps and licks hungrily bare bone,
enters like an unwelcome guest
into cracks and crevices vainly stuffed
with oily rags, wadded newspapers . . .
        Until a multitude of screeching
snowbirds whirl and wave above the frozen forests,
freezing beaks coaxing sterile succulence,
heralding the almost-ready rise of Spring.
Then all forces of nature stand poised,
a woman before her drawn bath,
tip-toe on the brim of warmth,
the gay splashings of life.

JUVENESCENCE

These townspeople picking in the trash appear
Soon after the college hobbledehoys commence
   summer;
Their fingers grasp something to encumber
Their rooms, some scavenged adolescent souvenir.

Barrels of discards stand weathering at the curb,
Filled with ephemera — pennants faded, guitars
   unstrung,
Phonograph records warped, alarm clocks
   unsprung.
The loss of things does not disturb

The youthful mind. Students leave behind
All they haven't room to pack or patience
To mend. And in their wake the insatiate
Middle-aged and elderly, the unresigned,

Descend like tramps in tatterdemalion dress,
Simple souls beggared by time.
They search for what the young gladly decline,
Pilfering what they can never possess.

PASTORAL

Bare toes toward heaven
a skinny lout lies,
bald eyes toward heaven
scan agate skies.

Bones of dry weeds
rattle at his move,
seed pods burst —
we coax the dust to love.

LATE SHOW

In drowsy silence we half-watch the screen
Where Dracula takes the Were-Wolf's mute bride
At twelve. Our pajama-clad boy beside
Us gapes with wonder: never has he seen
Bela Lugosi hypnotize his queen —
Celluloid fray of good and evil tried.
A few years ago our son would have cried;
Now, puts the poison with the fiend.

Knickers I wore to the dime matinee
Years past, when fanged Lugosi first kissed,
Betrayed, his beloved. Time can't delay
That act: still the monster keeps his tryst.
My simple son sees innocence fall prey,
A mean plot the growing seldom miss.

ROSEDALE AFTERNOON

The roses at white-columned Rosedale —
They were the most beautiful in the county.
And Sarajane, my daughter and only child,
The most beautiful of them all.
My mind has not forgotten.

On spring days I would wander
Through the arbor into that garden,
Nearly losing myself in the green maze,
The boxwood maze full of bird's nests.
The sun seemed to shine more then.

Spreading my skirt beneath the chinaberry tree,
My pink flesh alive as the plashing fountain,
Lolling in the garden, up to my thighs in flowers,
I sang the season's songs to the weather.
The roses are all withered now.

John Hubbard, my beloved, soon enough grew
    distant
And dismissed me in favor of the people of the state.
When he was forty he was made governor
And I had long before suffered an empty bed.
He was bright, but burned out like a candle.

Now I am, you might say, alone; the weather gray,
My clumsy hands are two cold stones.
Too easily I lose myself in that garden now,
John Hubbard's dust will not search me out,
And Sarajane is the town idiot.   •

TO AARON COPLAND

On His Sixtieth Birthday.   1960.

Suffused light focussed into brilliance of blazing
    poppies
Sprung forth full grown from sparse Appalachian
    soil:
You have given us adagios and allegros of feeling
    that soar
Over grazed grasses and glazed glasses of a nation
Balloon-bursting with joy and hysteria.
       Shaker, Quaker, farmhand, bigcity Jew —
All are here — sprightly, rightly denim dancing to
    the groan
And thwack of tractors and threshing machines.
Brazen henna-haired Jazz descends upon a New
    England town,
Assaulting the immaculate and austere moods of
    sunparlors
And hundreds of stingily-lit, yarn-filled sewing
    rooms.
       Ascend your podium, Maestro-Composer!
Give the tender land more — more ripe rhythms,
    plump
Music to pleasure a tinselled, troubled day.

WORDS FOR AMY LOWELL

"They laughed who later shouted praise
For my fruit shops, Chinese jewels,
My flower fragments, dragon scales.
Yet look, look what it all has brought:
Reflections upon reflections,
Word-nettings of wind, of silver,
Can now startle, sashay — then leap
Off the page straight to the mind's eye.
Sing my praises now if you will,
You sycophants and fawning fools;
But be brief as a soap bubble,
Concise as any grain of sand."

AUNT ELSIE

Aunt Elsie was an ancient kite:
  Tissue thin, her ribs the brittle sticks,
Drifting dumbly about with no destination,

Until the North Wind caught her up:
  It sucked the air from her feeble billowing —
She fell to the ground with a slight thud.

DANDELIONS

Tiny heads popping up, yellow as butter,
　　They encroach upon the world's front yard
And gather in gregarious lawn parties
　　Which seem to arrest the season.

Tow-heads together bobbing gaily,
　　Frail effulgence of hyacinthine curls,
Their life is a summer of festivals.
　　They think that they will live forever.

Yet soon enough light heads are grey,
　　In the first thin wind they scatter;
Year after year they teach us
　　How soon, how soon we disappear.

AUTUMN REMNANTS

That tarnished antique sun dimly gleaming
through smoke-smothered autumnal air
darkens daily with the charburning of time.
Clouding, deepening its dull-edged countenance,
it hangs, a cherished tea tray in the sky.

And we who wish to forget its increscent etchings
seek rushing waters still scurrying,
ponds not yet ice-scrimmed and silenced,
faint steam rising from child-like gurglings,
the churned water crisp and gossipy . . .

We search for brown maple boughs not yet barren,
caress the last lingering foliage fingers
to reluctantly clothed, frost-fearing bosoms.

ONCE UPON A STEEL COLD WINTER

Once upon a steel cold winter
in the mouse-gray envelope of dusk
we sat in a lighted parlor
and drank tea steaming from delicate cups.
More delicate than bone china were you:
Fragile bones outlined your giraffe-like neck,
the arch of your bowed back cut a line
cruelly into tight-stretched silk.
More slender were you than a willow branch,
branches that dally and dip their hands in spring
    pools,
drinking your mellow tea from exquisite bone china,
sitting in a wicker chair which stiffly creaked.

And then the razor-thin snow slid in,
Catching, clinging, building on the window sill;
you watched as I fondled your long fine hair,
hair that held an inner glow brighter far
than the sun's molten sputters, the moon's pock-
    marked silver.
You looked at me as I kissed your primly painted
    lips,
ringed your waist with warm, eager hands.
You trembled, the slightest bit,
a crisp dry leaf in autumn's fast breeze,
while the sounds of winter,
       all winters,
          closed in
             around us.

GREETINGS:

In tweeds somewhere he strolls across the sward,
His whole world enclosed, a campus courtyard;
Textbooks, tobacco, a slide rule in hand,
The docile, determined young man with plans.

And bright tomorrow will find him, surprised,
Stiffly curled in weeds under shell-shocked skies,
Belly ripped open wide like a cocoon,
Blue eyes empty and staring, a simpering baboon.

CRIPPLE

Like a lame beetle he lumbers along,
Hunched in his beetle-black coat.
How wretchedly he carries that leg,
A part of him he cares not to claim.
The sun burning through thickets
Magnifies and mocks his looming shadow,
His own gnarled limb distended.

A pool of sleek boys fiercely splashing
Calls up to him and forces a retreat —
"Crip! Crip! Crip! Watch the old crip go" —
The cries echo past the plaza where white pigeons
    coo.
They bore to his brain and fester.
Last year he caught a pigeon, and with a penknife
Cut the wings off even at the joint.

IN MEMORY OF ELIZABETH PURNELL

(d. 1961)

The sun of summer glared the same
    And bull-brave waves battered the shore,
Heat-rocked June, July, August came —
    She did not bathe as before.

She did not sit, survey the sea,
    Her golden ringlets wild-breeze blown,
Healthy limbs, tanned mellow as tea,
    A gay goddess on a sand throne.

Since summer last, grave winter fell,
    Subjecting her to dire repose.
She faded till I could not tell
    It was the same girl in a doze

So deep it seemed for days she dreamed
    In chill colder than June's first swim.
The radiators knocked and steamed
    Yet her blue blood froze to the brim.

She died before the solstice claimed
    Her winter-weary body prey;
A new Apollo had her name
    And lured Elizabeth away.

JOHN JACOBS DEPARTING

John Jacobs at dawn woke aguish and chilled,
Gathered prune-wrinkled garments one by one,
Tidied papers in a desk overspilled
Then slipped out to meet the day with the sun.

His lungs filled with the febrile humours of day
And his bladder burned from contents part stone;
Shuffling his feet in a determined way
He reached town with legs pain-riddled to the bone.

Jacobs had plans which only he knew:
Carrying his black Sunday-best to be cleaned,
He rested outside till the process was through —
Pinstripes pressed by rejuvenating machine.

Back home he saw the front gate aslant,
Nailed it plumb, making it stand to full height;
Stick-propped each drooping and bruised melon
    plant;
He died at midnight with everything right.

FIVE O'CLOCK A.D.

It was a day like any other:
  The balanced blue and green ball
Was spinning out in time,
  Spinning out in space;

Animals were whimpering unheeded in the cold,
  Newborn children cried in the dark;
Mr. Smith was slyly seducing Mrs. Jones,
  Country X clandestinely plotting
The overthrow of Country Z
  (Country Y having already seceded from the
    Universe);

When suddenly disturbing the air,
  Ponderously walking, swinging a chain
Of marvelous gold keys, came God, saying:

"It's closing time, Gentlemen.
It's closing time."

WRITER-IN-RESIDENCE

Schizoid poet, lumber up College Hill
Breathing like a dolphin, looking sad —
Too many bottles, too many pills,
Too little writing, too little, too bad.

The school you teach for, second-rate,
The pupils you preach at, dull.
Genius-in-residence, desolate,
Try to hold conference with fools.

Fawning Circes (wanting to be
Writers, not wanting to write)
Encircle you at smoky teas:
Bitches in heat, about to bite.

Your last book, last testament, ten years ago
Cool critics picked and sheared to shreds.
So smile for students, placate ego and Head,
Then homeward drag, to bottle, to bed:

In alcohol books get written,
In slumber fey critics swoon.
Bankrupt poet — gray, balding, stricken —
You wake haggard at dawn in some rented room.

URBAN NOCTURNE

Red neon reflections bleed noisily
on wet and slippery walks: the cries
of an old hag calling her scrawny cat;
tinny sharp music pierces jaggedly from a ragged
    cafe,
its sharp edges glinting at the curb, dangerously;
traffic squeals and screams like stuck pigs;
at night are best heard the sounds of a universe.
(Listen to Van Gogh's "Starry Night" explode,
    explode!)

Black fire escapes are cubist serpents wildly dancing,
torn newspapers dumbly flap, mute mouths
in the wind rushing between close-planted
    tenements . . .
While I, seated on my crimson-turned sooty window
    sill
look down upon brown iron shadows which rust
    before my eyes,
down upon the groined forest of nighttown,
and I caress the limp and livid geranium in my
    hands.

THE FALLEN APPLE

You sit before us, recondite and slight.
I cannot perceive your coming to harm.
Yet last month's newspapers in black and white
Molest you before the world's alarum.
They say it was a tramp or someone mad
That lured you by some candy saraband
Into the woods. Young eyes saw acts forbade,
Acts which older minds barely understand.

Your parents think it did you no great harm,
Infelicity to be forgotten.
They do not see that thin smile, full of charm,
You disarm me with: Awareness of men
Is in your eyes, your blood, my cherubim,
Eleven years old, devouring my limbs.

AT THE FIELD'S EDGE

After the churches' last stained windows dim,
Hungering night swoops down like a strident crow,
Circles with a dry cough that shivers bone
And wraps the fields in thick folds of black wings.
The sky, cacophonous, is loud with *Caws*.

Raucously they shatter the crystal air.
These seldom snowed-upon, confident fields
Now silver slated in the moon's dull sheen
Bear shoddy remnants of last season's crops
Like white beard stubble showing through.

This winter is the bleakest of winters
In a land of farmers with empty bins.
Sing loudly your hollow hallelujahs!
Bending, pray while the sun is prodigal —
Or fly in obscene circles with the crows.

CHANSON

Your beauty is the blossom beauty
Of the spice-spirited out of doors;
Your soft mouth sweet as nectar
From the ivory and gold honeysuckle
Which crazes bold striped bees in the sun.

When you are near I am a bee:
My clouded mind buzzes loudly, loudly,
My head spins in mad multi-colored circles.
I have no veil-veined wings to support me —
Stretch out your arms, white as cream,
That I may fall into the solace of your flowers.

DAEDALUS AND ICARUS

As they make the panpipe
Daedalus fashioned feathers on a frame,
Wax and reeds and eagle's feathers
For escape from his labyrinth.

Eagle's feathers and reeds and wax
He gave his son, too, saying,
"By water and land escape is blocked,
But the air, the sky, is still free!"

More than mere reeds, feathers, and wax
He gave: His words are with us yet.
"Keep a middle course over the sea,
Fly neither too low nor too high."

(Seaspray drenches downy wings,
The sun makes soup of wax.
What elders say, youth disregards;)
Icarus fell to the sea like a stone.

Daedalus the poet: His problem —
Transcend the walls of self.
Flight must be fraught with urgency
Into light, toward ideal repose.

Poetry is flight, rising on its strength,
Agile limbs proscribing an aspiring arc.
Neither soar into that searing plane,
Nor graze the banal sea's cold waves.

Icarus aimed to embrace the source.
His heart forgot his head.
Any flight to Sicily from Crete requires
From the whole man that last forbearance.

GOURDS

Four forms loll in the compote:
Plump Rubens nudes,
        round broad bottoms
Voluptuous and fleshy.

Seeds of a season preserved —
        Orange orbs! how you loved them
in the market, an orange afternoon.

They grace the table,
        bright blobs fixed in time,
ensconced now in space.

You will hate the gourds . . .
        When winter leers in your window
Autumn fruits are faded, infirm,

Wrinkled skins warty and dead.

WASHINGTON REFLECTION

The Father of his country?
This is inordinately clear:
For his monument we've erected
The largest phallus in the hemisphere.

PEELINGS

After sunburn I always peel.
First breaks in the skin appear,
Then flakes, falling in scatters
And tatters of confetti —

Mirthless aftermath of some Mardi Gras.
Gingerly I help slough off
Dead skin that once was me.
Each tug at the living edge quickens.

Quickly yesterday's color
Is gone. No vestige remains.
Would that we could shrive
Yesterday's guilt as easily.

SIX HAIKU

i

Awesome is the grove:
　　the birds perch on naked trees
　　like fat grey blossoms.

ii

The dim old poet writes
words to make him immortal,
leaves the wind blows away.

iii

When young I was sure
never ever to grow old . . .
Crows scream in my ear!

iv

Dead my laughing friends,
   dry my dreaming well, but still . . .
       Cherry blooms each spring!

V

The currents rush on,
carrying all broken reeds
away from the source.

vi

The day had been long,
    then I found you beside me —
      O! how short the night!

MAGIC

My magic apparatus, my bag of tricks,
rests in the basement now. A cotton-batting rabbit,
mystical linking rings, multiplying billiard balls,
vanishing silk handkerchiefs and feather bouquets —
the preoccupations of a childhood misspent —
beckon, Svengali-fashion, still.
The lure of chicanery remains.

Stored there, those pretty deceptions,
those fabulous feats of legerdemain,
should seem tawdry to me now.
All lacquer, gilt, and glitter can not conceal
the illusion of illusions. Only children deceive
and are themselves not deceived.
The adult mind discovers the trick.

Any day was a good day to practice
my magic. A corner of the attic was reserved
for the black table, its embroidered silver moons
ordered from some Philadelphia prestidigitator.
I was a moon gazer night and day.
Hours then disappeared for a boy
behind a necromantic table.

It didn't matter if the boy could not hit
a homerun, perfect a flying tackle.
Every day had a false bottom.
The mawking outside could not reach
that enchanted tower with its hagridden conjurer . . .

Ah, magician, charmer, pale wizard,
you practiced your tricks too well:

Sleight of hand must be outgrown.
Mere magic can not stay the mind.
The boy becomes a man of shop-worn tricks
in a world with no trap door.

CHILDHOOD FRAGMENT

Demurest of the tabby kind . . .
A Fav'rite has no friend!
— Thomas Gray

Because you always followed
The one you dumbly felt master
I carried you to the grocery store.
In my grip your heart beat faster.

You seemed my pet forever, Mickey,
Most constant belonging, vessel of trust.
Returning you fussed and clawed
When a white-walled Packard raised dust —

It frightened you to frenzy:
My hands loosened, you dived.
A quart of milk lay splattered
Where what was Mickey writhed.

That Packard soon was in another county.
But conscience does not so quickly rush
Away for a boy who owned, carried,
Allowed to let fall, be crushed.

Mickey, some nights I see you still,
Leaping before oncoming wheels, on my wall.

MOOD PIECE

Sadness of a barren tree,
Emptiness of old egg shell,
Quiet of mosses underfoot —
My heart between love's seasons.

A SONG FOR SIBYL

O sing a song for Sibyl
    Because she has such beauty
    And yet so fiercely grieves.

What was the Sibyl's answer
    To the old inquisitor?
    Simply this: "I want to die."

Why should Sibyl want to die,
    She with so much to live for,
    She having wisdom so great?

"If you knew all that I know,
    Had seen all that I have seen,
    You would not have to ask."

LOCH NESS

(for Robert Francis)

What is it that hugely moils these waters,
Diving while the gorse thrusts its yellow buds,
Pied wagtails and water-ouzels feed impatient
   chicks?
Each spring something flirts in the depths beyond.

The Scots know he's there: for thirty-three years
He's frolicked oddly in their green waters,
Snaking undulatory through the loch.
They'd make him patron saint, if they knew his
   name.

A few fools from the city try to capture him,
To take him in, on motion-picture film.
Theirs is a negative attitude.
He's never surfaced for a camera yet;

I don't expect him to. He's a slippery sort.
Scaly, and shy, too. All forty feet of him
(With a serpent's head!) scud the sea
Fast as factoried speedboats, opened wide.

Old sea captains see him with bald, unfailing eyes.
Every spring, at mating-time, they watch
Till awkwardly he scrambles toward Fort Augustus
Then back again, regular as any commuting train.

Will some wizened Ahab take to pitchy waters
To tackle that reeling, wily one-humped back?

Some fisher outraged at the reality of the unreal?
At night cruel hooks grab fishy guts upon my wall.

To the god of fishes I pray from my charred city:
Let him never be throttled, but enjoyed till graves
    gape wide —
A friendly monster, playing just beyond the shelf,
Beyond the reaches of reason.

TO AN ACTRESS PARALYZED AND DUMB

So many merely seem that way,
Feeble talents unable to portray
Great suffering, internal strife.
You are different. In this life

Your melancholy face on silver screen
Is thrown in Rome and Muscatine.
You have caused the world to feel,
Through make-believe, tragedy's reel.

Now tragedy's real, and I weep annoyed
Not for gestures struck on celluloid
But cosmic strokes which seem to clout
Like thunder, to put your life to rout:

Patrician face flash-frozen like a fish,
Nimble tongue now thick and whist;
Even your children's lives seem fey,
To terrible fates they've fallen prey:

One died in the night from measle's licks,
Another's sweet brain is hydrocephalic —
Head hashed in some taxi's path
When baby's carriage rolled into its wrath.

What misery's left? Mestrôvic's *Job* is solid
Bronze, squats on dung, toad-like, squalid,
Tortured tongue distended, silent stone —
Suffering and shock hugely hone.

Still Job was someone in a Book.
Today we cannot comprehend that look

Until the press has journalized your toils,
Pungent sorrows, pricking boils.

You seem misfortune incarnate,
And I can only wonder in what state
You worked your will, hideously:
Did you in Rome's circus laugh to see

Christian babies with lopped limbs,
Lionized since elders sang sweet hymns?
In Atlantis or Egypt, whip with tongs and tongue
Olive servants serving well, suffering long?

Sin from past lives the present profanes.
Only karma can keep me sane.

TWELVE VERSIONS OF
THE MAN ARCHIBALD

I

Rhythmically rowing across the horizon
He doesn't know the squinting girl picnicked ashore
Translates him into Adonis, lithe in the sun —
His parenthesized back so strong (but sore!),
Arms pulling mightily in the tide's slew,
Legs long and muscled (but varicosely blue!).

II

Loose dandruff flaked on a knobby red pate.
That's all the barber knows of Archie Shuttlethwaite.
That, and acquired esoteric knowledge
Of Archie's cowlick, which he clips like a hedge.

III

Comfort and solace in a cold winter's bed.
Warm flanks downed with fur foxy red.
Belly-button spills out (not sunken in).
Smells of fish and sweat, tobacco, moccasins.
Rises straightway at six regardless of weather.
One ball hangs a little lower than the other.
Sunday Bible readings by dim Mazda light.
Sheets wet every third or fourth night.
Teeth grinning from a glass on the bathroom shelf.
Insists upon rinsing his underwear himself.
In summer dotes on corn, tomatoes, and berries.
This much she knows of the man she married.

IV

To Doctor Suture, Archie is a successful spinal tap
And buttocks that quiver like Jello, buttocks pale
as pap.

V

Some parishioners seem Simon pure, some blackly
smirched.
Old Archibald? That shadow rarely darkens the
church.
When it does, ushers observe a niggardly giver.
No complaint: his boat's useful. We baptize at the
river.

VI

Christ that man is sloppy!
Wish I'd never bought this property.
That place next door? It's nothing but a sty.
I'm ashamed to live here when folks drop by.
Never rakes his leaves the whole year round.
Overrun with rats. Them howling hounds
Dig my petunias, leave calling cards
Which I step in all over my yard.

VII

A black horsewhip swishes through the air.
My clothes are off. Pappa has a crazy stare
As he beats and beats me till he falls tired.
My back patterned and welted like a waffle iron.
It was raining when I left, lame and raw.
Hate in his eyes — that's the last thing I saw.

VIII

The soul of kindness, the way he treats them hounds
And waits on that saintly wife when she's down.
Last year he nursed a crippled mallard till it healed,
Then let it go near the marshes past Whaley's field.

IX

Greasy wallet bulging in his pocket, a spendthrift
    wife,
Never gave *me* a penny's business in his life!

X

The only blood relative I know.
The only inheritance I could receive —
If that wife of his is quick to go.
His coat needs mending at the sleeve.

XI

The pebbles roll like thunder down my tin roof.
    Snuck
Away from that whining bitch. Midnight. She's
    asleep.
Unlatch the back door and in 'Baldy creeps.
He jazzes me better than most Niggertown bucks!

XII

Shuttlethwaite? His time seems to be soon.
Slight shamble in his walk, voice out of tune.
Just wait. Soon enough he'll meet my terms,
Let me lay him out, powder his face, give him to
    the worms.

HAPPY, CRAZY AMERICAN ANIMALS
AND A MAN AND LADY AT MY PLACE

*(after the painting by John Wilde
in the S. C. Johnson Collection)*

A portly possum dangles by his tail
From my livingroom rafter. He adroitly assails
Reality from topside, where inquiring crows nest.
The fox in stony stance upon my chest
Of drawers looks stuffed, but his bark of love
Is such stuff as dreams are made of.

Brilliant-hued birds and somber bats
Fly overhead. Underfoot a domiciled wildcat
Bats a ball across my planks, beneath my eaves,
But those furry forepaws' claws are sheathed.
The panoplied armadillo has seized
Upon shards of a vase which once I prized —

Oh, the vanity of earthly possessions!
The vase was broken in the animals' procession
That toppled my turvsy vanity upon its side.
Which is real? The fox and armadillo, or I?
I think there's a leopard behind that door.
The back door is open still. Are there *more?*

A polar bear lurches to embrace me like a brother.
Wild ducks fly in one window and out the other,
Following an inner weather I cannot know.
My house is modest. The plaster falls like snow.

It was my sanctuary, legacy for kin.
What kinship with these beasts, clamoring in?

Antediluvian arteries pulse in time and quick
With those of a naked lady, prime and pink,
Now prancing in step with the great horned stag;
The beat of their marching does not lag,
Parading princely across cracked linoleum.
Something in her high society succumbs.

All out of doors wants in, all in of doors out.
Something wild in the mildest of us shouts.
These creatures, sniffing in strange civility, would
Huddle close and comfort us, if they could.